THE RUNNER

The Runner

Christopher Morris

The Runner
first published 2020 by Scirocco Drama
An imprint of J. Gordon Shillingford Publishing Inc.

Scirocco Drama Editor: Glenda MacFarlane

Cover design by Doowah Design
Author photo by Tim Leyes

Printed and bound in Canada on 100% post-consumer recycled paper.
We acknowledge the financial support of the Manitoba Arts Council and The Canada Council for the Arts for our publishing program.

Production inquiries, please contact:
christopher@humancargo.ca

Library and Archives Canada Cataloguing in Publication

Title: The runner / Christopher Morris.
Names: Morris, Christopher, 1974- author.
Description: A play.
Identifiers: Canadiana 20200173499 | ISBN 9781927922576 (softcover)
Classification: LCC PS8626.O75725 R86 2020 | DDC C812/.6—dc23

J. Gordon Shillingford Publishing
P.O. Box 86, RPO Corydon Avenue, Winnipeg, MB Canada R3M 3S3

For Yakov Mueller.

Christopher Morris

Christopher Morris is a playwright, director, and actor, and is the artistic director of the Toronto-based theatre company Human Cargo. Past writing credits include *The Runner* (Human Cargo / Theatre Passe Muraille – 2019 Dora Awards for Outstanding New Play and Best Production), *Our Beautiful Sons* (Blyth Festival 2017 and 2012 Playwright in Residence), *The Road to Paradise* with co-playwright Jonathan Garfinkel (Human Cargo / Crow's Theatre / Buddies in Bad Times Theatre), *Night* (Human Cargo / National Arts Centre, published by the Canadian Theatre Review / Canada Playwrights Press), *Return: The Sarajevo Project* (co-playwright with Sue Balint, Daryl Cloran, Alena Dzebo, Holly Lewis, Tanya Smoje and Dylan Trowbridge, Theatrefront, Dora Mavor Moore Award nomination, published by Canada Playwrights Press). Christopher lives in Toronto with his partner Gillian Gallow and their daughter Eileen.

Acknowledgements

The Runner flourished under the guidance of director / dramaturg Daniel Brooks. His insight, patience, and persistence were empowering. Thank you, Daniel.

I'm also grateful to all the individuals / organizations who've helped me during *The Runner*'s creation and premiere: Judy Zelikovitz, CIJA, Francis Mueller, Hinda and everyone at Ein HaNetziv, Noam Shalev, Ruti Barkai, Samer Shalabi, the Al-Akhras family, Howard Rypp, Ishai Golan, Signe Katz, David Weinberg, Rabbi Yehoshua Pfeffer, everyone at the Z.A.K.A. office in Jerusalem, Marwan Athamneh, Natasha Greenblatt, Andy McKim, Regine Cadet, Jefferson Mappin, Alexandre Alexandrov and Marina Stefanovic at Broadview Place, Joel Beddows, Judy Farthing, Ada Aguilar, Remington North, Jane Johanson, Graham Isador and the staff at Theatre Passe Muraille, Amy Matysio, Kat Gauthier, Tyrone Savage, Lucy Peacock, Kevin Bundy, Andre Morin, The Stratford Festival, Craig Pike, Phyllis Berck, Sylvia Morris, Linda Gallow, Ron Minken and Natasha Krestinina, Bryan Gallow and Anthea Boyer, Rob and Wendy Kadlovski, Tara Niccodemo, Hillary Guertin, Paula Schultz, Michael Rubenfeld and Selfconscious Productions, Robert Massoud, Razi Shawadeh, Alon Nashman, Jonathan Garfinkel, Norm Morris, Gillian Gallow and Eileen Morris.

We acknowledge the support of the Canada Council for the Arts, the Ontario Arts Council, and the Toronto Arts Council. Nous remercions le Conseil des arts du Canada de son soutien, le Conseil des arts du Ontario, et le Conseil des arts du Toronto.

Playwright's Note

I want to create theatre that explores the extremes of the human condition. I'm interested in what happens to us when we are pushed to our spiritual, moral, and emotional limits because it's at these times that we see the best, and worst, of what we are.

The Runner focuses on the pushback a Z.A.K.A. member experiences when his devotion to serve others – regardless of their race or creed – clashes with the divisive beliefs of the community around him. As we slide further down the path of political and social division, now more than ever, we need to champion those who put human decency above tribalism while knowing full well the consequences they'll face.

This play is dedicated to Yakov Mueller, a Z.A.K.A. member in Israel who passed away in February 2018. He first welcomed me into his home in 2010 and over the years we spent many hours talking about the experiences he had working with Z.A.K.A., from the harrowing to the profound. He was my beacon of light as I navigated the murky currents of this play. Yakov was a beautiful soul, full of compassion and self-deprecating humor. While passing away from cancer, he was surrounded by his loving family and friends, and in death was shown the same tenderness and care he offered to so many.

With love, Yakov, thank you.

Christopher Morris

Foreword
by Ishai Golan

A foreigner lands here, in a land in which he is a guest, a tourist. Arrives to a region different from his home in almost every parameter imagined. He spends a fairly short amount of time here and yet has the audacity to write a play. It is audacious because the play he writes is not about him or his personal experiences during his visit; on the contrary – the play is an intimate, deep, personal monologue spoken from the point of view of a local. And not just some generic local, but rather a very specific and unique individual, a character full of complexity and contradictions that reflect all the dialectic powers and layers of his surroundings and upbringing. A very ambitious attempt that might be seen as courageous – or perhaps foolish. Either way, it has resulted in one of the most relevant, exposing, dramatic, intriguing, and unique texts concerning contemporary conflicts and life in Israel. A view of Israel so sharp only a fresh set of eyes could spot and unfold it.

I have no police or professional military background apart from my three-year mandatory military service as an actor in the IDF Theatre Corps. I am a simple, peaceful citizen born and bred in Israel. How many people do I know who have died in war or acts of violent terror? A few, but even a few in this regard is far too many. Life in this part of the world is a ticking bomb. Anxiety is the national anthem. Z.A.K.A. is yet another element in our rich texture of life in Israel. For us living here, it is simply another fact of life, like the existence of grocery stores, ambulances, and firefighters; we have Z.A.K.A. volunteers who appear at every tragic site to collect the flesh and blood remaining at the scene.

I find the primal allegory of this play rare in its accuracy: the hero's destiny is to face as many ticking bombs as he can, but he always finds them moments after they've exploded, and has to retroactively defuse them. When I initially met this text, I had one of those striking, tingling shocks, like hearing a great song for the first time in your life but feeling like you've known this song for years. I immediately tried to remember where I had met this character. In what play, movie, or TV series? I couldn't believe that the idea of telling a story from the perspective of a Z.A.K.A. volunteer had never been explored in Israeli drama. Probably because it was too close. And it is a dramatic gem for numerous reasons:

- The position, the idea of a Z.A.K.A. worker, is exotic.
- The Z.A.K.A. volunteers are always chasing action.
- Diving into the world of Z.A.K.A. is waltzing with death, and death and devastation are the oxygen of drama.
- The people of Z.A.K.A. are obsessive, committed, spiritual, traumatized, sensitive, and competitive – what more can a playwright ask for?
- The ongoing crisis in the Middle East is a playwright's playground.

This dramatic gem has been here under our noses all along and we couldn't see it.

Jacob is a fictional character; he does not exist in real life. And so how is it that I know him? Why do I identify with him? He revives long-lost memories, shadows, Israeli characters who are constantly hidden, you know them but you've never looked twice, never stopped and truly observed them. This play puts them centre stage, and through their perspective we learn about ourselves and the place we are living in. That is the power of theatre and the extraordinary power of this play.

Ishai Golan
December 2019, Tel Aviv

Ishai Golan is an Israeli actor who has been acting in theatre, TV, and film in Israel, and outside of it, for the past 30 years.

Production History

The Runner premiered on November 29th, 2018 in Toronto, Ontario as part of Theatre Passe Muraille's 2018/19 season. A Human Cargo Production, with the support of Theatre Passe Muraille.

Cast

Starring GORD RAND as Jacob

Creative

CHRISTOPHER MORRIS – Playwright/
Human Cargo Artistic Director

DANIEL BROOKS – Director/Dramaturge

GILLIAN GALLOW – Set/Costume Designer

BONNIE BEECHER – Lighting Designer

ALEXANDER MACSWEEN – Composer/Sound Designer

JUDY FARTHING – Stage Manager

ADA AGUILAR – Assistant Stage Manager

REMINGTON NORTH – Production Manager

DEVON JACKSON – Producer

ERIC DIZON – Publicity Designer

LYON SMITH – Production Photographer

The Runner has also been presented during the 2019/20 season by The Socrates Project in Hamilton, Ontario (September 2019), the Grand Theatre in London, Ontario (November 2019), and by the Tarragon Theatre in Toronto, Ontario (February/March 2020).

Jacob (Gord Rand) recovers after being knocked off his feet. (Photo by Graham Isador)

Jacob (Gord Rand) describes the scene of the stabbing in Jerusalem. (Photo by Gillian Gallow)

Jacob (Gord Rand) describes finding a mass grave in the Ukraine. (Photo by Christopher Morris)

Jacob (Gord Rand) embodies his brother on the settlement. (Photo by Graham Isador)

Characters

JACOB, a man in his forties.

Setting

Jacob exists in a dimension between life and death.

Notes on Text and Production

Punctuation, or the lack thereof, along with the spacing of lines on a page, are purposely placed for the actor and director to discover the rhythm of the performance. This proved useful in our first production. I say this, however, knowing that each performer, director, production is unique.

When Jacob "runs" in the script, this can be interpreted as each production sees fit. The original Human Cargo production was set entirely on a twenty-four-foot-long treadmill which was constantly in motion, from barely perceivable to a speed that required actor Gord Rand to run at high speeds.

Darkness.

The lights flicker.

We see JACOB, a man in his forties.

He's running.

He's wearing black shoes, black socks, black pants, Tzitzits, white dress shirt, fluorescent Z.A.K.A. vest and a black kippah.

He runs with focus, determination.

He passes through shadow, light, darkness. It's turbulent. A world of shadows.

JACOB: What's happening, what's happening, what's happening?

Why can't I remember. Why can't I remember what. Why can't I remember what happened. Why can't I remember what happened to. Why can't I remember what happened to me. Why can't I remember what happened to me right. Why can't I remember what happened to me right before. Why can't I remember what happened to me right before!

There is a deafening, surreal sound.

JACOB's body physically responds to this.

It pummels him, knocking him off his feet.

JACOB starts shaking uncontrollably.

I'm wet, I'm wet…why am I wet, I'm not wet…how come I feel wet? I'm cold, it's cold.

He struggles to stand. Eventually he's able to.

Pause.

Why can't I stop shaking…stop shaking. It's okay you can stop. It's okay, stop shaking. It's okay, everything's going to be…you can do it. Everything's going to be okay, everything's going to be okay, everything's…

JACOB paces for a while, trying to gather his thoughts.

What's my name?

Pause.

My name's – come on! My name's…I live in Har Nof with my mother, her name is…my mother's name is – come on, what's her, what's my mother's…?

Pause.

I pick up body parts at bombings, car accidents, that's what I do. I put the bodies together, every piece of skin, every drop of blood…why…why… Jews need to be buried whole…

Pause.

JACOB looks at the vest he is wearing.

Z.A.K.A., Z.A.K.A., I work for Z.A.K.A.! That's what I do, I'm a good person, I work for Z.A.K.A.

Pause.

JACOB searches through his pockets.

Where's my, where's my phone? They can't, if they can't reach me, they need to reach me, they have to be able to call.

Pause.

Was there an attack, is that what's happening here, is there a body? Something bad is happening. I can feel it. Something very bad is happening right now, there's an emergency, somebody's dying, I can feel it, somebody's dying, right now!

Pause.

Is this about the Arab girl, is that what this is? Is that why I'm here, the Arab girl? Is that what's going on?

Pause.

The Arab girl?

Pause.

Okay, the Arab girl, okay…I arrived at the scene, before everybody else. Lying on the road was a dead Israeli soldier. Stabbed to death. Thirty feet away was the Arab girl, lying face down. Dying. Between them was a kitchen knife with an eight-inch blade, an eight-inch blade with a black plastic handle, a black plastic handle that snapped when it hit the soldier's collarbone, I saw it, I was there when I walked past the soldier who was dead, to the Arab girl. But was it hers, was that knife really hers? Everyone thought it was hers, they always think that, but in this case, in this particular instance I didn't know, it was never proven, they couldn't prove it, I don't know if she stabbed that soldier.

She was lying face down on the pavement, she was shot in the back, gasping for breath, she was drowning in a pool of her own blood, I turned her over, her face was a black sopping mess, I used my finger, my index finger, with my index finger I moved aside the wet black hair splayed across her face, like I was removing a hair out of a cup of milk, like I was removing a hair out of a cup of milk with my index finger…full mouth, soft nose, her eyes, rolled back in her head, she started to convulse, she was convulsing –

One, two, three – Breathe!

One, two, three – Breathe!

Coughed up a river of blood,

Gushed into my mouth,

I swallowed,

Blood rushed down my throat,

One, two, three – Breathe!

She stabilized,

My hands started shaking,

My stomach rolled,

I swallowed her blood,

I ingested,

I contaminated,

She contaminated me.

She contaminated me!

Pause.

Did you know that the girl started crying, they didn't write that in the papers, did you know that she was scared? I think she was scared, I don't know, she was in pain, she was crying, why was she crying, because she thought she was dead and wished she wasn't? Because she knew she was alive? Did she regret what she did – you see, even I do it, I just did it, why do I think she's responsible? I don't know if she stabbed that soldier, all we know is that people shot her when she was running away, but does that make her guilty, guilty because she was running away, maybe she saw it happening and ran because she was scared? Did she deserve to be shot in the back for that?

She was lying on the pavement, beside me, crying, she's a person, a teenager, a girl, what was I supposed do, sit beside her, sit down beside her? It didn't make a difference, she didn't even know I was there, I didn't even know if she could hear me, maybe she had hearing issues –

"Hey! Hey, hey hey! Can you hear me?"

She cried harder, she groaned, her hands started flailing, I grabbed hold of them so she didn't hurt herself –

"You're going to be okay," I told her,

I didn't know if she would, what's okay?

"You're going to be okay" I told her,

Her hands softened in mine –

"You're going to be okay,"

She turned her head to me, cried, squeezed my hands –

"You're going to be okay, you're going to be okay, you're going to be okay..."

Pause.

The Z.A.K.A. team arrived at the same time as the ambulance, the paramedics tried to push past the Z.A.K.A. team – they do that they'll push us out of the way "Stick to the dead!" they say, we're trained in First Aid – so Yossi, the Z.A.K.A. team leader, pushes one of them back and says "If you got here faster we wouldn't have to do your work for you!" there's more pushing and shoving, people start coming out of their shops and homes to see the dead soldier, the Arab girl, lying in the street, the knife, everyone crowded around us, the paramedics cut away the Arab girl's shirt, her injured breasts exposed for everyone to see, so I said to them, "What's wrong with you, do you have no respect, can't you help her without humiliating her – you don't serve God, you people!" I take off my vest to cover her up and the crowd of people started pointing at me saying "That's the guy who saved her, him, that one right there!" pointing at me, somebody threw a half-drunk can of Coke at the girl, it bounced off the road beside her spraying all of us, and this big rabbi pushed his way forward, cuffed me on the side of the head and screamed at me, "Shame on you for saving her! Shame!" The police pushed him and the crowd back, the paramedics threw the girl in the back of an ambulance and she was taken away.

Alive.

Alive.

She was alive.

Yossi walked right over to me, poked his finger into my chest, hard –

"What's wrong with you?" he asked me, just like that, *"What's wrong with you?"* He's Russian.

"What do you mean?"

"That Arab girl," he said, "what's wrong with you?"

He shook his head and pushed past me.

What's "wrong" with me? I did something "wrong" by saving her? I saved her life! We all swore the Hippocratic Oath, *he* swore it, to serve the person with the greatest need, it removes all bias, it makes the decision for us, no matter what a person has done or *might* have done, we swore to help them, to *not* do that is murder, did he want me to commit murder, to kill that girl?

Pause.

Then the Z.A.K.A. team started collecting the soldier's blood from the road, looking for any pieces of skin, and they didn't wait for me, they didn't wait, they turned their backs to me, they wouldn't let me reach the soldier, that's never happened before. These four "stars" of Z.A.K.A. get asked to do all the interviews on TV, have these perfect lives and perfect jobs, one of them's a mechanic, one has an international shipping company, another has a kosher bar, and Yossi, the "number one" star, has an online Judaica Superstore – but I don't have another job, I'm on call twenty four/seven, if I sleep my phone's under my pillow, I don't have time to do anything else, this is all that I do, this!

Yossi's watching over this new kid in training, it was the kid's first time on the job and from the look on his face it was the first time he'd ever seen a breast – shredded and dripping blood – probably never even spoken to a girl before, he was turning grey, and Yossi slapped the kid on the back and said right in front me – "Have you ever drank before?" – I've done how many jobs with them thirty, forty, Mr. Titless has done one – I've seen lots of breasts before living ones not just the ones on the job *real* ones, in magazines, but I've never touched a breast in all my life – that's a choice I've chosen not to do that – but why did he invite the kid, Yossi didn't invite me out after my first time, we washed our hands on the side of the road with a bottle of water and left our separate ways – why didn't he invite me, why the kid?

The "stars" eat sauerkraut, potatoes, and chicken, and they drink vodka, every time after they work, the same meal, at the same restaurant, every time – they have a special "bond" and they sit at their "special table" in the back – it's always available, I don't know if they call ahead or maybe it's because the owner loves them so much he kicks out whoever's sitting there the second he sees them waltzing through the door. And that night they filled the kid up with alcohol, I saw them from across the street, and food, they sang, they shook him by the arm, messed up his hair, laughed when he coughed on a cigarette, were quiet when he cried, then grabbed him and shook him again to make him laugh, and I knew what they were laughing about, it was really funny – Yossi's a really funny guy, I really like him when he's like that, then they finished their meal, staggered out, arms around each other, soaked in sweat, laughing and singing, they weren't even aware it was raining, and the kid could barely stand and the guys laughed even harder and they all staggered up the road, back to their perfect homes.

I went into the restaurant and sat at their table before it was cleared, put my hand around the oily finger prints on Yossi's glass, could see his lip marks, the grizzled chicken bone and cartilage on the plate, the warmth of his seat, the smell of his sweat, I took a menu like I was in a hurry but knew exactly what I wanted – "Give me the same as them!" I barked at the waiter, "and leave the bottle!" It was half-drunk, I wasn't going to drink it I kept it out for the smell, the waiter quickly came to clear the table and in an instant wiped away all the life and energy that was just sitting here moments before and in a second it was gone – just like that – and all that was left was the odd grease smear on the table and I was cold I was freezing my clothes were soaking from the rain the heat in the restaurant made it worse and the food was terrible my mother's is better and she was alone at that moment sitting at the table with a hot meal she just cooked waiting for me to come home and I choked on a piece of chicken that wouldn't go down the smell of vodka made me want to puke and the waiter didn't ask he didn't ask how the food was nobody in the restaurant looked at me nobody asked me why I was shivering, nobody cared nobody called, nobody calls my phone, nobody calls me.

Why?

Why don't they call?

Why doesn't anyone call me?

Pause.

When I got home that night, my mother, she was sitting there with a cold plate of dinner in front of her, and I'd just eaten at the restaurant, I wasn't hungry, how could I eat, how could I eat twice? I can't eat twice.

Pause.

"You're never here anymore," that's what my mother said, "you're never here anymore, you're always working, I don't hear you come in at night, you leave before I wake up, the only way I know you've been home is if there's pee on the toilet seat, why don't you lift the seat, you never eat the food I leave you, I live alone, your brother Ari doesn't call, no one calls me, I'll be dead for days before anyone would know and then you and your Z.A.K.A. people will come and zip me up in a bag, you'll spend more time with me dead than when I'm alive, do you want me to die before having grandchildren? I want grandchildren, Jacob, is that so much to ask!"

She has grandchildren, my brother Ari has kids!

"But you don't have any, Jacob, why don't you have any children? You won't even let me buy them little toys, or clothes that I see on sale – Mrs. Hertzel has nine grandchildren – *nine* and her son Moshe has a clubbed foot, he had no problem finding a girl – what's wrong with you, why are you doing this to me, do you want me to suffer, am I not good to you, do I not make you every meal, wash your clothes, am I not a good mother to you, why won't you give me grandchildren, what have I done that makes you hate me so mu – "

She started rubbing her calves, she's so fat she can't reach her feet, she has problems with her feet, but does she wear the shoes I bought her or the circulation socks, no no no no no, she wears these cheap plastic sandals and old, tearing polyester nylons that don't breathe, they stink, her feet stink, like sour milk, and when I took her stockings off to rub her feet, this, knobby, cauliflower, bloomed in my hands, and when I squeezed, her metatarsals rippled between my fingers, I could feel the pulse in her foot, twitching in my palms, and it was like I was holding her life in my hands, I'm holding my mother's life in my hands – she needs to see a doctor.

"No doctors!" she screamed. "No doctors! I know a girl, her name is Leah, a widow – but with lots of energy! She has some kids, seven kids."

I'm not going to marry her, Mummy, or fertilize her eggs, never! Can't she guess, doesn't she know, that it's never going to happen?

"But typical of you," she said, "you've already ruined it! Leah told me something about you Jacob that I'm ashamed to say in this house, that she heard, that she heard you, that you, that you have an Arab girlfriend, an Arab? Leah said that, 'Jacob has an *Arab* girlfriend!' How could you do this to me, an *Arab*, how do you have an Arab girlfriend!?"

She's not my girlfriend! I said.

"So you know this Arab – "

She's a client!

"Then call Leah and tell her, that she's confused, that she got it wrong, that you would never do that, lie if you have to, Leah just moved here, she doesn't know anything about you yet, this is your only chance why do you want to ruin it!?"

JACOB starts walking quickly, then running.

Less than five hours after the Arab girl was thrown in the back of the ambulance, my mother's talking about it at our kitchen table, the Arab girl got inside our house, my mother, she polluted our kitchen, we can't eat there any more it will never be the same, how can it ever be the same, and it doesn't matter that it's some twisted version of the truth, in less than five hours – *five hours* – it spread through the crowd through my neighbourhood through "Leah" directly into my mother's ear, poisoning her mind, poisoning her opinion of me, nothing I say could ever change her mind about this, my mother's scared of Arabs, even before we moved here from England she'd cross the street if she saw one coming, and she thinks I have an Arab girlfriend, it's over – my mother, my house, my home, our home, permanently destroyed in less than five hours! For what? I'm a good son! I've always been good to her! My mother, she's important to me, she's all I have! This is the thanks I get for being a good person, for saving that Arab girl's life!?

There is a deafening, surreal sound.

JACOB's body physically responds to this.

It pummels him, knocking him off his feet.

JACOB is shaking uncontrollably.

I'm wet why am I wet I'm not wet how come I feel wet?

He struggles to stand.

What happened? What happened?

Pause.

Why can't I remember what happened to me right before?

Pause.

What happened to me right before here…

Fire hydrant…

White car…

Bus stop…

White car crashed into a bus stop…

I'm wet…

T, t, t, t, t, t, t, tearing tearing tearing, tearing, tearing, nylons – nylons, tearing nylons, tearing nylons – my mother, is it my mother, did she fall, is she okay, where is she, is she trying to call, what if she's trying to call, Mom! Where are you?! Mom!

Pause.

JACOB looks around at his surroundings.

What is this place?

Where are we?

Where am…where am I going?

Why am I talking?

Why am I even talking to you?

Am I hallucinating?

I'm dreaming. This is a dream. It's a dream.

Pause.

My mouth touched her mouth, I swallowed the Arab girl's, stop thinking – she's not my girlfriend! – how can I have an Arab girlfriend, my mouth was on her, but that doesn't make me, she's an Arab, I don't like Arabs, I don't like them – I don't mean it like that, I was brought up that way, I don't associate, our paths, I would never marry an Arab – an Arab *girl*, I mean I can't, I don't dislike Arabs some of them are handsome, I just don't know any Arabs, men or women, I don't know any outside of work, okay I won't say "Arabs," Arabs, Arabs, they're Arabs I can't won't call them Palestinians, they're stateless they don't have a country, it's not bad to call them Arabs, they're "Arabs" – okay okay okay I won't say it, I won't call them that anymore, I won't. I won't do it. I won't do it.

Pause.

I saved her life, okay? I *helped* her, it shouldn't have even been up to me to make a decision about whether she lived or not, God is supposed to make decisions like that, not me, so why didn't *He* save her? Does He not "intervene" in these kinds of situations, but it's just up to us to sort it out, but He punishes us in the end if we get it wrong? Ah yes, "when God breathed life into our nostrils He gave us goodness," so we all share a divine goodness, so if there's a universal "goodness" guiding us through these situations, why are we so cruel to each other, why is everything so complicated?!

JACOB sings "Delilah."

(Singing.)"My, my, my Delilah…"

My father.

(Singing.) "Why, why, why Delilah…"

My father – "Johnny Friendly" – big round belly, beautiful mouth, greased-back hair, gold rings on every one of his pudgy fingers, cigarette dangling from his hand holding the microphone, pint of lager in the other, singing the "Oldie b'Goldies" down at the pub, women threw their underwear at him, I saw it – Mrs. Zelikovitz from up the road…

When he was dying…

He grabbed me by the hand and told me that he wronged me. Wronged me? Said he was sorry for never "accepting" me, and promised, that for as long as he lived, he would see me for exactly who I am… and he did, for the last three days of his life…didn't hurt a soul his entire life and there's this big, beautiful man on his deathbed, purging his conscience of his one sin so he can stand before God and face His Judgement…why am I talking about my father?

Pause.

What was I talking about? Think. Think think think, okay… the night I saved the girl, the restaurant, my mother, everything that happened on that crazy night, okay that's everything that happened on that night but what happened next?

Pause.

The only thing I remember, the Ukraine…the Ukraine…?

Pause.

Okay, the Ukraine...Z.A.K.A. got a call from a Jewish organization in the Ukraine, who were convinced there was a mass grave on a piece of land that had just been sold to a developer, but it had never been proven, so the builder gave them three days to sort it all out and after that the condo was going up, so they called Z.A.K.A. to go there and dig it up and Z.A.K.A. sent me to do it – see, I remember all this clearly – if people were in a mass grave they were murdered, they were buried without dignity, so I went there, I flew to the Ukraine right away and dug and dug and dug for three straight days, started finding skulls, and femurs, and clothing, unearthed the remains of two hundred and eighty-three women and children, two hundred and eighty-three Jewish women and children, larger skeletons lying beside the tiny skeletons of their children, one clean bullet hole bored into every skull.

Pause.

Okay, so, the job was to line up the skeletons in rows, before putting them into their coffins, but there was this, there was...a larger skeleton that had its arms wrapped around a smaller skeleton, the job was to separate each individual skeleton...but...this mother, she had her arms wrapped around her child, her daughter, she died holding her daughter...How could I do it, how could I separate them? I couldn't even touch them, I just stared at them...

Pause.

What did that mother think when she looked up at their killer, with her arms wrapped around her daughter? What do you think at a moment like that? Did she go before her daughter, God willing, or maybe she wanted her child to go first, to spare her daughter the horror of seeing her mother being murdered. To spare her the feeling of terror before she died. I bet you this mother did everything she could to calm her child, to help her not be scared, to let her daughter know that she loved her, that she'll always love her, that they'll always be together, that she'd be there…I honoured that mother and her child, I honoured their love. I took off my gloves. Their bones…I laid them down together…

But right away, right away I thought, who did I do that for, they're dead, I'm the one walking away from this, it was all for me, I got the highest form of mitzvah two hundred and eighty-three times, they couldn't thank me, it's the highest form of mitzvah to do a deed I can't be thanked for, I can't be thanked.

Who collects mothers and children from their homes, walks beside them, ignores their crying and pleading, forces them into a pit onto other bodies, points a pistol at them and pulls the trigger – who does that? How can someone stare into a child's eyes, an innocent, and extinguish their life? What's missing in the people who do this? Is there some innate goodness in us that's corrupted, or is this our natural state, a barbarism that takes years of bludgeoning and taming in the hopes that one day we might act with grace? Is that why life is so exhausting? Are we just animals? And if their killer, if that piece of – was in front of me right now, lying on the ground *dying*, pleading for me to save his *life*, I'd save him, in an instant. And would that mother and daughter have let me touch their bodies, even *look* at their embrace, if they knew I would treat their killer with the same tenderness and respect I was giving them now? Have I no principles?

Have that going through your head when you're digging up a mass grave! It never stops, every single thought, every scenario is the Arab girl – sorry, the girl – her eyes, her mouth, her hands, saving her… holding her…

When I got back from the Ukraine, there was no way I was going back to Jerusalem, to my mother, to the girl, do you know what it's like to spend days in the cold damp air at the bottom of a mass grave and step out of Ben Gurion airport and smell the hot scented air blowing through the palm trees? I'm not going back to cold, rainy Jerusalem, I wasn't expected home for another day, and it didn't help that the *sherut* driver to Jerusalem had a fat, pockmarked face and barked like a dog when he spoke, and that directly to my left was a shiny new taxi headed to Tel Aviv with a young driver with his little bum leaning against the hood in faded, tight blue jeans…I'm not going to skip this detail…I knew that he could take me right to the door, in less than thirty-one minutes I could be at the door, so I slid onto that young man's black leather seat, jerked forward into the dark, humid night, smelt his cologne, our eyes locked in the rear-view mirror, I was thinking did he know where he was taking me, had he been there before, had he seen me there before? So I said, "Don't look at me thank you," and he smiled back at me with thin, wet lips, he was smiling, why was he smiling?

My phone rang, it started ringing, I didn't have to look at it, I didn't, why did I have to see who was calling, I rolled down the window, stuck my head out into the hot humid night, salt spray from the crashing waves on the beach kissed my lips, I was a spirit, drifting through a humid world, a world I shouldn't be in, that didn't know I existed…and through the door I went –

He passes through darkness, and flashes of dim light.

I stripped down to my underwear and shoes.

Walked across the dance floor.

Two men in their fifties stopped dancing as I approached.

The bald one put his hand on my arm.

It was electric.

He locked eyes with me.

I met his gaze.

But looked away and kept walking.

I was going to the dark rooms.

I walked down a dark, narrow hallway.

Passed through a wall of warm, musky air.

Into the darkness.

The sound of slapping skin.

Sporadic groans.

A flicker of flame as someone lit a joint.

Flashes of men.

It was a pile.

Of bodies, arms, legs, wrapping around each other, twisted.

It was a tangle of writhing men.

We crowded like bulls in a pen.

Backs of hands brushed across my groin.

Someone squeezed my testicles.

My lower back was sprayed.

Men spilled and spat on the floor.

Sweating, slopping, squeezing into each other.

And there was no judgment.

There is no judgment, there is no judgement, there is no judge –

Silence.

Nobody knows me there.

Who I am.

Nobody cares.

I'm normal…I'm normal.

Pause.

He was killed when I was in the taxi to Tel Aviv, that twelve-year-old boy…okay okay okay okay okay, focus, think, what happened…

An Arab – protester in Ramallah was shot and killed by an Israeli soldier. The next day, for revenge, his brother broke into an Israeli settlement, climbed through a bedroom window, saw an innocent, twelve-year-old Jewish boy sleeping in his bed… and stabbed him twenty-seven times – *twenty-seven times!* Z.A.K.A. called to tell me about it, on my phone they called but I didn't I couldn't I was in the taxi to Tel Aviv the one time I didn't answer, they had to leave me a message about this boy, about little Ishai – I called Z.A.K.A., they told me he was in an ambulance – "Keep him alive!" I said "I'm on my way, keep him alive! Don't call the death keep doing CPR, keep him alive!" When I arrived at the hospital they said it was too late, that Ishai died in the ambulance on the way over, that he was gone, that twelve-year-old Jewish boy was gone… if I answered my phone, if I reached him first, if I went back to Jerusalem, he'd be alive…is this my punishment, am I being punished for that? Is the world, fate, God punishing me for who I am, punishing that child for what I did with those men, does the world actually function like this?

And when I walked out of the hospital there was shooting – gunshots! And I see this Orthodox man holding his arm, he had blood spreading across his shirt saying, "I've been stabbed, I've been stabbed!" and then this Israeli guy runs over, waving a gun around saying, "A terrorist stabbed this man and ran up the sidewalk, so I shot at him, I didn't mean to, I'm sorry – I was shooting at the terrorist, I was shooting at the terrorist, I didn't mean to shoot her!" and up ahead on the sidewalk was the Israeli woman he accidentally shot and a man crouching over her shouting, "He shot her, he shot her, that guy just shot my mother!" And he did! Just as I was walking out of the hospital, just after seeing the body of little Ishai, this Israeli guy shot and killed that old Israeli woman – we're killing each other, why, why, why are we killing each other now!?

JACOB starts walking quickly, then running.

It's not normal to live like this. "But we're finally in the Holy Land, with our own government, running our own lives," but is this better? Nobody wants us here, all this violence, all the humiliation we inflict to carve out this tiny strip of land, to push back all of our neighbours who want to annihilate us, it's not normal. Then go back to where you came from they say, you mean where my people fled to when the places we called home turned into places we had to run away from, where exactly do we go back to, this is where we started, this is it, this is where we began, here, so do we all run from here now because it's gotten too dangerous for us, it's never going to end, it's never going to stop!

It's not normal to live like this, it's not normal, I have ulcers, colitis, prone to cystic fibrosis and it's not all the in-breeding in the Jewish community this is an evolutionary response to our impending annihilation! We're porous, the threat of violence, it's airborne, it gets inside of me, I feel it! I can feel it!

There is a deafening, surreal sound.

JACOB's body physically responds to this.

It pummels him.

JACOB fights to remain upright and accomplishes this.

Pause.

What's happening?

Pause.

What happened to me right before,

Before *here…*

Pause.

Fire hydrant, white car crashed into a bus stop, I'm wet, tearing nylons…a baby…was there a baby?

Pause.

Was that my fault?

Is that why I'm here?

There is a deafening, surreal sound. JACOB's body physically responds to this.

JACOB speaks with pace and drive.

Okay, I understand, soon after the hospital, Yossi called me and told me I had to dig up the bodies for the Goldberg exchange, it wasn't my idea, the government was releasing one thousand and twenty-seven convicted terrorists from jail and returning the remains of thirteen terrorists in exchange, for one, *one* living, captured Israeli soldier, for Goldberg. Z.A.K.A.'s official line is that they collect the remains of terrorists to give them back to their families, but we don't give them back to their families we give them to the Israeli authorities to be buried in shallow graves with no religious rites, no dignity, to be dug up later and used as barter in exchanges like these – it's inhumane what we're doing, it's not Jewish!

So, Yossi picks me up in the middle of the night, we drive for hours – doesn't say a word to me the entire time – we arrive at a military base somewhere in the north, the soldiers at the front gate wave us through, and up ahead, in an area lit by a small floodlight, are thirteen brand-new wooden coffins, waiting to be filled.

Yossi and I put on our rubber gloves, protective suits, face masks, we start digging and right away Yossi's shovel thumps the lid of a coffin below, it's weightless as we lift it from the ground, we open it, and inside there's just a few small bags, bloated with gas, infested with maggots, black with rot, I don't know if it's a man or a woman, if they're young or old, what they did, what their names are, they're dead now, turned to nothing, the result of an act of violence, that's all they are now, meat for barter. We place the bags on top of the pristine white sheets that line the sterile new coffins, that will be carried through the streets of Gaza under roaring AK-47's.

Then Yossi turns to me and says: "She's being released tomorrow, as part of the exchange."

Who is?

"Your Arab girlfriend."

Good, she shouldn't be in prison.

"How do you think that soldier's family feels?" he said, "the soldier she killed. That she's alive and'll walk free tomorrow, while their son is dead, how do you think that makes those parents feel?"

The only thing that came to mind…was that we swore an oath, that's what I said, we swore an oath to do no harm.

There is a deafening, surreal sound. JACOB's body physically responds to this.

JACOB speaks with pace and drive.

The head of Z.A.K.A. called me in, he wanted to see me –

"Jacob, sit down!" the Head of Z.A.K.A. said, directing me to an empty chair in front of his desk. Yossi's there too, wearing the same dirty clothes from when we dug up the bodies last night.

"There's something I want to say you, Jacob," the Z.A.K.A. head says, "and it's important you hear it from me first, personally, before it's announced. We're going to make some changes to our triage practice. From now on, when Z.A.K.A. responds to attacks, we'll treat the victims first. Victims *before* the terrorists. Do you understand? If the terrorist is in most need of medical attention, you help them *last*."

Help the *Arabs* last, I say.

He folded his hands, "We would save any victim, Arab or Jew, that's not what I'm talking about, the terrorists, Jacob, you have to help the terrorists last."

So, just let them die? I asked.

"Why should a second of triage be spent on someone who purposely hurt others? These terrorists want to die, so you're not helping them by saving their lives, 'Let Death steal over them; let them go down to Sheol alive; for evil is in their dwelling place and in their heart!'"

Are you doing this because I saved the girl? I asked.

"Jacob. You need to take some time off, talk to one of our therapists, and after, if you come back, you can serve us in some other capacity, like vehicle maintenance, or filing – "

But...what will I do? What am I supposed to do with myself...? You're hypocrites, you know that? Animals, you're fucking animals, let them die!?

There is a deafening, surreal sound. JACOB's body physically responds to this.

JACOB speaks with pace and drive.

He fired me, okay! The Head of Z.A.K.A. fired me! I got fired from Z.A.K.A.! I was fired.

So I drove to my brother's house on the settlement, and that was a bad idea, when my brother opened the door, all he said was, "Why didn't you tell me you were coming?" not how are you, long time no see, and then he brings me around to the back of his house, not through the front door, but to the back into his office where he hustles his customers, not into his home, his place was freezing.

Why don't you turn on the heat? I ask him.

"I pay for my electricity," Ari said, "I work for a living, not like you and the other twenty-five percent of the population that don't pay taxes, praying doesn't turn the heat on."

Then he checks his cell phone and says, "Come on."

He takes me outside onto his driveway and standing beside Ari's car is this chubby, Korean evangelical with manicured hands folded over his Bible, wearing pressed khaki pants, his short-sleeved golf shirt buttoned right up to his throat, a grey brush cut; a polished, repressed, sixty-year-old man-child.

"Long time no see, Ari!" said the Evangelical, hugging my brother, then he squeezes my arm, "Ari is very special person, he loves Bible, he is good man, are you good man?"

Ari pops open the trunk of his car like a drug dealer, and it's overflowing with all the videos he makes about the historical/religious significance of "Samaria," where he lives, and how it's the geographical setting for the coming Apocalypse. The Korean Doomsdayer rifles through the pile of movies like a kid in a candy store, then holds one up – "*The Fire is Coming! Will you be Ready?* Great title, Ari. I'm ready!" then he slapped me on the back and said, "Are you ready?" and laughed and bought twelve of them, muttering "praise Jesus, praise Jesus."

Then we went driving on the settlement because the Christian Apocalypse wanted fish and chips and was going on and on and on about fire and the impending war that was coming, and I'm rolling my eyes and my brother's giving me dirty looks in the rear-view mirror and Ramallah's on the other side of the settlement's security fence, towering over us, and I say, I couldn't help it, I said, "How can you live so close to them, Ari, to the people you hate?" so he takes a sudden sharp turn, speeds recklessly down the street and says, "I want to show you something, Jacob."

Then the three of us are standing at the visitor lookout for Jacob's Rock, where Jacob supposedly laid his head to rest and dreamt he saw a ladder in the sky with God at the top and angels ascending and descending between heaven and earth, when God supposedly told Jacob that as far as he could see, from the north to the south to the east to the west was the land of the Jewish people and He promised that He'd bring us back to the land, *this* land, to Israel, and I look around, and I think, this? He gave the Jews this place? Cold, miserable, rocky hills, no oil, no resources, *this*?

And Ari said, "Thirty-five hundred years ago we were expelled from here by *force*, and after thirty-five hundred years, within the framework of the most just and moral process that has ever occurred in the world, we've returned home. I am living the dream that our grandparents, our great-grandparents, our *ancestors* could only have dreamt of. We are the lucky generation and I embrace my role in the historical drama that I am a part of and I feel *lucky* to be rebuilding the Jewish people in our ancestral homeland. And there's only three ways for this to go for the Arabs around here: those who want to accept our rule can accept, the ones who want to leave can leave, and those who want to fight can fight, but we'll defeat them. Every encounter between a soldier and enemy must end with an unequivocal decision. It ends. It hurts. It's meaningful. You don't belong here, Jacob, you shouldn't be here."

Oh really, so where am I supposed to go?

"Go back to London! Where you don't have to follow the word of God, where you can roll your eyes and criticize the *real* Jews! You're a coward, Jacob, moving here will never change that. Dad wouldn't have lasted here either – the fucking two of you – people like you, you're the kind of Jews that have no business being here – why? – because you're the ones who bow down to them, to the Arabs, the kind of Jews who are ground to dust under their feet. You live at home, you're not married, you don't work, you don't pay taxes! You have no moral or financial investment in the future of this country, you're a vulture, you circle around waiting for bad things to happen and if nobody's hurt or dies, you starve – you even *save* them, you told me yourself! That cunt who stabbed the soldier, they shot her, she was dying and you brought her back to life, she's just been released after serving only seven months, and you'll be responsible for when, not if, *when* she kills again, because she will. How can you look at yourself in the mirror? You don't know what it's like to lose a friend, a neighbour, you don't see the children who wake up in the morning with nightmares, I live that, every day of my life, this is not an abstract enemy that I am facing, he throws stones at me on my drive home and I have to live inside the settlement behind a fence because he's going to penetrate this settlement, climb into my window and stab my fucking wife! You wanna live with that?"

Then why do you want to live here, Ari?

"Because it is mine, Jacob, it's mine!"

There is a deafening, surreal sound. JACOB's body physically responds to this.

JACOB speaks with pace and drive.

All right, all right! I needed to see her, *her*, the girl, I had to see her!

It was the town in the second valley, that's what I was told, that's all I knew, "She lives in the town in the second valley," then up ahead, a minaret, covered in gaudy green lights, old stone buildings – this is the town where she lives – the car barely squeezed through the narrow streets, people were looking in my windows, they weren't used to people like me there – "It's the blue metal door beside a butcher shop," that's what I was told, that's where she lives, "The blue metal door beside a butcher shop," and then I saw it, up ahead, the butcher shop, scrawny, greying meat, swinging in the sun, swarming with flies, that's it that's where it is, and beside it, beside it, the blue metal door.

Pull over! Get out! Is the car running, I don't know, keys in the ignition? Come on! My gun, put it in my belt! I know how to use it I know how, of course I know how to use it! Bang on the door, don't knock on it, bang on it! Bang again, do it again! Here they come, the whole town stay calm stay calm, they're crowding around me, bang on the door, bang it again!

It opens –

Pause.

JACOB slows the pace of his speech.

It's her.

I look at her.

Standing in front of me.

The girl.

Shiny black hair.

Soft nose.

Full, wet mouth.

"What do you want?" she says.

She doesn't even know who I am.

But I can see her.

I can see her.

I fall on my knees.

Crying?

I'm crying?

She puts her hand on my shoulder – "Are you all right?"

I'm weeping, shaking, the noises coming out of me, I can't stop, a water bottle's pushed in my face – knock it away, people start arguing with each other, somebody pulls me up, who's pulling me? Let go! Let go of me! Some guy's pulling me to my car, opens door, bangs on my hood and says – "Go, go, get out of here! Drive! Go on! Go! Go!"

Pause.

Her hand on my shoulder.

Are you all right.

That's all that matters.

Kindness.

An act of kindness.

Pause.

A male voice can be heard reciting a passage from Psalm 91.

This passage is repeated multiple times, underscoring JACOB's following text, and abruptly ends when there is the deafening sound of clearly defined gunshots.

(Prayer:) "For He will instruct His angels on your behalf, to guard you in all your ways. They will carry you in their hands, lest you hurt your foot on a rock. You will tread upon the lion and the viper; you will trample the lion and the serpent. When He calls out to me, I will answer Him; I will be with Him in trouble. I will deliver and honour Him."

Hello? This is a prayer for the dead, I can hear you praying! The dead can't hear you, I can hear you, I'm alive, I'm still alive, thank you!

JACOB starts walking quickly, then running.

Okay, so you think my soul is hovering above my body, on the "cusp of Judgment," is that what this is about, is that why I'm here? You think I lived a bad life, that my soul is caught in a thicket of thorns? That my soul is being pulled through a thicket of thorns? I lived a good life, I deserve an easy death, so my soul's passage is like removing a hair out of a cup of milk with your index finger. I want that one, with the milk and the hair, the easy one! Give me that one! I want the easy one! I want that one!

There is a deafening sound of clearly defined gunshots.

JACOB's body physically responds to this.

He remains upright.

Long pause.

JACOB discovers the following events as he speaks them.

Right before I got here,

I was in Jerusalem,

It was right after I saw the girl,

I went for a walk,

And saw a white car crash into a bus stop full of people,

It happened right in front me,

Knocking over a fire hydrant,

Cold water was roaring under the car,

I ran over,

Felt the water gushing around my ankles,

Up my shins.

The coldest water I ever felt.

The driver pulls his head from the steering wheel,

Stunned,

His foot's still pressing the gas,

The engine revs,

There are bodies lying in the bus stop,

A woman stares at a large piece of metal,

Tearing through her nylons.

Someone starts screaming "My child! My child!"

Pinned between the white car's bumper and the bus stop is a pram,

Shivering under the force of the engine,

I can hear a baby crying,

See a leg sticking out of the pram,

People are shouting, "The terrorist is still in the car!"

They start shooting,

Filling the car with holes,

Close to the pram.
I'm standing in front of the car,
Looking down at the baby in the pram.
Bullets whistle by my ear.

Pause.

I'm staring at the baby.

I freeze.

I can't move.

I don't help.

I don't help the baby.

Pause.

They shoot again.
The driver's head pops.
Spraying the windshield red.

I feel heat.

My chest burns.

My head snaps.

I fall back.

Cold water takes my breath away.

I feel pain.

I'm lying on my back.

But I'm standing.

Yossi runs by me.

I turn to see where he goes.

He runs to me.

Lying on the ground.

A bullet hole in my chest, my head.

I've been shot.

Yossi starts CPR.

He touches my body.

He's touching me.

But I'm standing here.
I hear everything people are saying.
I try to speak to them.
But they can't hear me.
See me.

I want my mother.

I walk up her stairs.
My legs are disappearing.
I go through the wall.
I'm in her kitchen.
She's at the table, waiting for me to come home.

I'm a ball of energy.
I'm engulfed in light.
There's energy around me.
Strands of energy.
Look at it.
Flowing through us.
Through everything.
I know this.
I've known this energy for thousands of years.

And I…

Am…

Pause.

What happened to the baby?

Pause.

JACOB starts to run, slowly at first, then faster.

He passes through shadow, light, darkness. It's turbulent. A world of shadows.

I want to go back.

I want to go back.

I want to go back.

I want to go back.

I want to go back.

I want to go back.

I want to go back.

I want to go back.

I want to go back.

I want to go back.

Blackout.